Never Forget the Difference you've Made

Empire

PRESS

Printed in Great Britain
by Amazon

64137510R00058